CW01659098

Rannaghor

Rannaghor

Roopa Sharma

Rupa . Co

Text Copyright © Roopa Sharma 2006

Published 2006 by

Rupa . Co

7/16, Ansari Road, Daryaganj, New Delhi 100 002

Sales Centres:
Allahabad Bangalore Chandigarh Chennai
Hyderabad Jaipur Kathmandu
Kolkata Mumbai Pune

All rights reserved.
No part of this publication may be reproduced, stored in a retrieval system, or transmitted, in any form or by any means, electronic, mechanical, photocopying, recording or otherwise, without the prior permission of the publishers.

Cover and Book Design:
Peali Dutta Gupta & Vivek Dutta Gupta
Photographs: Sirish Sen
The Studio, D4/4232 Vasant Kunj.

Printed in India by
Gopsons Paper Ltd.

CONTENTS

Introduction

Bengali cuisine – a term synonymous with good food, plenty of fish and desserts! What is not, perhaps, so well known is that it has a vast bank of vegetarian dishes, has tremendous variety in terms of taste, and is healthy because of the use of much less oil and spices as compared to, say, North Indian or Rajasthani food.

There is, today, a renewed interest in Bengali cuisine, as seen from personal experience. And that is the motivation behind this collection of recipes. I hope I have achieved what I wanted to – to bring to you the simple yet rich and diverse taste of Bengali food.

This book is dedicated to my mother not only because she shared her fabulous recipes for this collection, but also because she was instrumental in making me start again when I had given up after the initial burst of enthusiasm.

Friends and family have all helped and encouraged me in my endeavour. This book is dedicated to all my well-wishers who encouraged me in this work; to my mother and mother-in-law from whom I learnt cooking; to my daughter and husband, Ujjainee and Pranay for their encouragement; to all those who always appreciated my cooking – especially my in-laws and my sisters, Ratna and Rita.

Poribeshan
PRESENTATION

Most readers will agree that it is easier to cook a meal than to decide WHAT to cook. I have, therefore, presented the recipes in combinations for a meal, rather than as 'stand-alone' recipes.

A traditional Bengali meal will consist of:

- **Bhaat (Rice)** — the staple cereal of Bengalis. Rice is normally eaten as plain boiled rice. Variations are pulao and 'ghee bhaat' (fried rice).

- **Teto (Bitters)** — the first course in a meal. It is either fried or cooked in 'shukto' – mixed vegetables with bitter gourd.

- **Shaak Bhaja aar Kasundi (Greens with Mustard Sauce)** — the greens normally used are spinach or 'kolmi shaak', and in winter red saag.

- **Dal aar Bhaja (Dal with Fries)** — dal is accompanied with a fried fish or vegetable.

- **Torkari (Vegetable)** — as indispensable as the fish! One or two vegetable preparations are a must.

- **Aamish (Non-vegetarian dish)** — the staple non-vegetarian protein of Bengalis is of course, fish; mutton, chicken and egg are eaten occasionally.

- **Chaatni (Chutney)** — a sweet and sour (khatta-meetha) ending to the meal. It is normally made with tomato, green mango, pineapple or raw papaya.

- **Mishti (Dessert)** — the obvious ending for a meal. It could be sweet (mishti) or plain yoghurt, kheer or anything from an immense range of traditional Bengali sweets – roshogolla, pantua, sandesh, and so on.

Bengalis eat their food one course at a time in the order given above. If you have planned a sit-down, then serve the food in the above order. In case of a buffet, you may guide your guests about this.

Our grandmothers and mothers spent a major part of their lives in the 'Rannaghor' (kitchen), preparing elaborate, time-consuming and delicious meals for the fussy and discerning family. But today full-time working wives/mothers, nuclear families, lack of help at home, paucity of time and health consciousness, have led to simpler and healthier eating habits even amongst us diehard foodies!

The menus range from simple to elaborate ones – for everyday and weekend cooking or for parties. You pick according to your mood or requirement!

Note:

- The quantities of oil mentioned in the recipes are for cooking in non-stick cookware. In case of normal cookware add about 2 tsp. more.

- Bengali cuisine traditionally requires all the ingredients – fish, meat or vegetables – to be fried before making the curry. I have dispensed with it except where absolutely necessary. This cuts down on oil consumption and cooking time. Sauté the ingredients for 2-4 minutes instead of frying.

- All the recipes here are for 4 persons. You will need to increase/decrease the quantities proportionately.

Nimontron
Invitation

The menus in this section are for traditional, elaborate Bengali meals, drawn up for the special occasion.

Party Menu I

This is a traditional menu, suitable for lunch.

Bhaat	Boiled Rice
Musoor Dal aar Aloo Bhaja	Masoor Dal with Crispy Fried Potato
Aloo Phoolkopir Dalna	Potato and Cauliflower Curry
Pabda Maachh Shorshe	Fish (Pabda) Curry with Mustard
Tomator Chaatni	Tomato Chutney
Bhaapa Doi	Steamed Yoghurt

BHAAT

INGREDIENTS

Rice	250 g
Water	3-4 cups

METHOD

1. Wash the rice 3-4 times under running water and soak for 30 minutes.
2. Put the rice and water in a vessel. Cook on a high flame and bring to boil.
3. Lower the flame and cook till done. If you are cooking basmati rice, you should turn off the fire before it is fully done. This will prevent the rice from getting soggy and overcooked.
4. Drain the water.

◆ ◆ ◆

ALOO BHAJA

Crisp and golden, this is a hot favourite with children and grown ups alike.

INGREDIENTS

Potato	500 g; peeled and cut in fine juliennes or coarsely grated
Salt	To taste
Red chilli powder (optional)	A pinch
Oil	For deep frying

METHOD

1. Wash the potatoes 3-4 times in plenty of water so that the starch is washed out. If not, the potato won't become crisp on frying.
2. Add salt to the potatoes and set aside for 10 minutes.
3. Squeeze out the water released by the potatoes.
4. Heat the oil in a deep wok (karhai).
5. Fry the potatoes in small batches on a medium flame. Stir constantly to prevent them from forming lumps.
6. Remove with a slotted spoon when they are crisp and golden yellow in colour.
7. Drain off the excess oil on paper towels.
8. Serve as an accompaniment with dal.

MUSOOR DAL

This is probably one of the most commonly eaten dals.

INGREDIENTS

Masoor Dal (red)	$\frac{1}{2}$ cup
Water	2 cups

METHOD

1. Wash the dal well in sufficient water.
2. Pressure cook the dal. Allow two whistles on a high flame.
3. Remove from flame and allow to cool.
4. Temper the dal.
5. Serve hot with plain rice and fries.

Tempering (Tarka) the dal:

Onion	1 medium size; finely sliced
Green chillies	4-5
Coriander leaves (optional)	1 tbsp.; finely chopped
Salt	To taste
Oil	$\frac{1}{2}$ tbsp.

1. Heat the oil.
2. Add the onions and fry till light golden in colour.
3. Add the boiled dal, green chillies and salt.
4. Bring to boil.
5. Turn down the flame and let it simmer for a couple of minutes.
6. Remove from flame and garnish with chopped coriander leaves.

◆ ◆ ◆

ALOO PHOOLKOPIR DALNA

INGREDIENTS

Cauliflower	1 large; cut into medium sized florets
Potato	2 large; peeled and cut into 8 pieces each
Tomato	1 large; finely chopped
Ginger paste	1 tbsp.
Green chillies	4-5; slit length-wise
Fresh coriander	1 tbsp.; chopped
Cumin seed	½ tsp.
Bay leaf	2
Turmeric powder	¼ tsp.
Cumin powder	1 tsp.
Chilli powder	½ tsp.
Oil	3 tbsp.
Ghee (optional)	1 tbsp.
Salt	To taste
Sugar	2 tsp. or according to taste
Water	¾ cup or as required

METHOD

Grind together:

Cloves	3
Green cardamom	5
Cinnamon	inch piece

1. Wash the vegetables well and rub in ½ tsp. salt and keep aside for 5 minutes.
2. Heat the oil in a wok and add cumin seeds and bay leaves.
3. Add the vegetables and sauté over a medium flame for 3-4 minutes.
4. Add the ginger paste, turmeric, cumin and chilli powders.
5. Continue to fry on a low flame till the masalas are well fried. Sprinkle a little water if the masala tends to burn.
6. Add the tomatoes, ¼ tsp. salt and 1 tsp. sugar, stir well and cover.
7. Allow to cook for a few minutes more till the tomato is soft.
8. Add the water, adjust salt and sugar and bring to a boil.
9. Lower the flame, cover, and let it simmer till the vegetables are cooked, but slightly crunchy.
10. Add the powdered clove, cardamom, cinnamon and ghee.
11. Adjust the quantity of gravy, garnish with fresh coriander and green chillies.
12. Serve hot with plain rice.

Variation: You can replace cauliflower with parwal – peeled and cut in one inch pieces.

PABDA MAACHH SHORSHE

Fish cooked in mustard gravy.

INGREDIENTS

Fish (Pabda)	4 medium sized; cleaned and washed
Yellow mustard	4 tsp.
Turmeric powder	1 tsp.
Salt	To taste
Mustard oil	3 tbsp.
Onion seeds	A pinch (Kalojire)
Green chillies	3-4; slit length-wise
Coriander leaves	1 tbsp.; chopped
Water	$^3/_4$ cup; or according to gravy required

METHOD

1. Apply $^1/_2$ tsp. turmeric powder and 1 tsp. salt to the fish and keep aside for 15 minutes.
2. Wash and grind together the mustard seeds, $^1/_2$ tsp. salt and 2 green chillies, to a fine paste.
3. Heat 2 tbsp. oil in a flat-bottomed wok.
4. Fry the fish lightly in batches on a high flame.
5. Discard any leftover oil, and heat the remaining oil.
6. Turn down the flame and add the onion seeds. When they splutter, add the mustard paste. Add $^1/_2$ tsp. turmeric powder and fry for 2-3 minutes on a low flame.
7. Add water, salt to taste, green chillies and bring to boil.
8. Lower the flame, add the fish and allow to simmer till the fish is cooked through. Normally pabda cooks in 3-4 minutes.
9. Garnish with fresh coriander and a few drops of mustard oil and serve hot with plain rice.

◆ ◆ ◆

TOMATOR CHAATNI

This chutney is easy to cook and good to eat too.

INGREDIENTS

Tomato	250 g; washed and chopped
Panch phoran	1/2 tsp.
Salt	1/4 tsp.
Sugar	4 tbsp. or to taste
Oil	1/2 tsp.

METHOD

1. Heat the oil in a wok and add the panch phoran.
2. When they splutter, add all the ingredients.
3. Cover and cook on a low flame till the tomatoes are cooked. Stir occasionally to prevent sticking/burning.
4. Removc cover, check on the seasoning and consistency of the chutney.
5. Serve chilled in summer or at room temperature in winter.

Variations: You may add about 15 g raisins or 25 g dates seeded and coarsely chopped.

◆ ◆ ◆

BHAAPA DOI

INGREDIENTS

Condensed milk	1 can
Thick sour yoghurt	400 g
Raisins	15 g
Almond	15 g slivered
Water	1 can (use the condensed milk can as measure)

METHOD

1. Empty the condensed milk into a large bowl.
2. Add an equal quantity of water to dilute it.
3. Add the sour yoghurt and mix well, using an egg beater/hand mixer, to get a smooth mixture.
4. Add the raisins and pour the mixture into a container with a tight fitting lid.
5. Place in a pressure cooker – without the weight – or a steamer and cook on a low flame for 30 minutes.
6. Allow the vessel to cool.
7. Garnish with the almonds and serve chilled.

Party Menu II

This is an elaborate menu, suitable for lunch or dinner on a winter's day.

Ghee Bhaat	Fried Rice
Luchi	Puri
Maachher Chop	Fish Chops
Bhaja Mooger Dal (Niramish)	Moong Dal (Vegetarian)
Chhanar Dalna	Paneer Curry
Chingri Maachher Malai Curry	Prawns in Coconut Milk
Tomato Amshottor Chaatni	Tomato Ampapad Chutney
Notun Gurer Payesh	Rice Pudding with Gur

GHEE BHAAT

Bengali 'Ghee Bhaat' or fried rice is mildly aromatic and a little sweet to taste.

INGREDIENTS

Basmati rice	250 g
Ghee	3 tbsp.
Cloves	2
Cinnamon	1 inch piece
Bay leaf	1
Raisins (optional)	15 g
Green chillies	8-10
Salt	1 tsp.
Sugar (optional)	2 tsp.
Water	3 cups

METHOD

1. Clean, wash and soak the rice for $\frac{1}{2}$ hour. Drain the water and keep aside.
2. Heat the ghee in a heavy bottomed or non-stick pan.
3. Sauté the washed raisins for 2 minutes. Drain and keep aside.
4. Add the cloves, cinnamon and bay leaf, and sauté for a minute.
5. Add the rice and sauté for 2 minutes.
6. Add the water, salt and sugar.
7. Cook until the rice is done and all the water is absorbed.
8. Add half the raisins and green chillies and mix well.
9. Garnish with the remaining raisins and green chillies and serve hot.

◆ ◆ ◆

LUCHI

The luchi, most Bengalis will insist, is very different from the North Indian puri. These are made from maida, and smaller in size. It may be served with any dry preparation of chicken, mutton, egg or selected vegetables – curried or fried.

INGREDIENTS

Flour	500 g
Ghee/Refined oil	50 g
Ghee/Refined oil	For frying
Salt	$^1/_2$ tsp.
Water	As required

METHOD

1. Make a stiff dough with the flour, ghee, salt and water and keep aside (covered) for 2 hrs.
2. Divide the dough into small portions, the size of lemons.
3. Roll each ball with a little dry flour into discs, about 3 inches in diameter.
4. Heat ghee/oil in a deep wok.
5. Deep fry the discs one at a time. Take care that they do not get burnt.
6. Drain off excess oil on kitchen towels, taking care not to puncture the puris.
7. Serve hot with dal or paneer curry.

◆ ◆ ◆

MAACHHER CHOP

INGREDIENTS

Fish (Katla/Surmai)	500 g
Potato	200 g; boiled and mashed
Lemon	1
Onion	200 g; finely chopped
Ginger	$1^1/_2$ inch piece; finely chopped
Salt	To taste
Sugar	2 tsp. or to taste
Cumin powder	2 tsp.
Chilli powder	$^3/_4$ tsp.
Garam masala powder	$^3/_4$ tsp.
Turmeric powder	$^1/_2$ tsp.
Bread crumbs	For coating
Egg	2; beaten
Refined oil	For deep frying

METHOD

1. Wash and drain the fish well.
2. Apply lemon juice and keep aside for 10 minutes. Wash again and drain well. Apply salt and turmeric powder.
3. Fry the fish on a medium flame till cooked through.
4. Remove skin and bones and mash the fish.
5. Heat 3 tbsp. oil in a wok.
6. Add the chopped onion and ginger and fry till the onions are light brown in colour.
7. Add the mashed fish and fry for 3-4 minutes.
8. Add the chilli and cumin powders and continue to fry till the masalas are cooked and the mixture begins to brown.
9. Add the mashed potato, mix well with the fish and fry for 2-3 minutes.
10. Add the garam masala powder, blend well into the mixture and cook for 2-3 minutes more.
11. Remove from fire and allow to cool.

To make the chops:

1. Divide the mixture into 10 equal portions.
2. Shape them into oval/round chops.
3. Dip each chop in the beaten egg, then coat with the bread crumbs and put away in a paper-lined tray.
4. Refrigerate for at least 4-5 hrs or overnight.
5. Deep fry on a medium flame till deep golden brown in colour.
6. Place on paper doilies in a serving dish.
7. Garnish with potato wafers and serve with ketchup.
8. Serve hot as an accompaniment with fried rice.

◆ ◆ ◆

BHAJA MOOGER DAL

INGREDIENTS

Yellow moong dal	100 g
Shelled peas	½ cup
Ginger paste	1 tsp.
Green chillies	3-4 slit
Grated coconut	2 tbsp.
Bay leaves	2
Cumin seeds	⅓ tsp.
Oil	1 tsp.
Salt	To taste
Water	1 cup

METHOD

1. Roast the dal, wash, drain and keep aside.
2. Pressure cook the dal with water – allow 2 whistles.
3. Cool and open the cooker and add the peas.
4. Cook again – this time turn off the gas after 1 whistle.
5. When the cooker has cooled, open, add the ginger paste and mix well.
6. Heat the oil in a wok.
7. Add cumin seeds and bay leaves.
8. Add the boiled dal, salt and green chillies, and bring to boil.
9. Lower the flame and let it simmer for a couple of minutes.
10. Garnish with grated coconut and serve hot with luchi.

◆ ◆ ◆

CHHANAR DALNA

INGREDIENTS

Paneer	250 g; cut in 1 inch cubes
Peas	$\frac{1}{2}$ cup; shelled
Potato	1 large; cut in $\frac{1}{2}$ inch cubes
Tomato puree	2 tbsp.
Ginger paste	1 tbsp.
Clove	2
Green cardamom	4
Cinnamon	1 inch piece
Turmeric powder	$\frac{1}{4}$ tsp.
Chilli powder	$\frac{1}{2}$ tsp.
Cumin powder	1 tsp.
Raisins	10 g
Cashews	10 g
Oil	2 tbsp.
Ghee (optional)	2 tsp.
Salt	To taste
Sugar	2 tsp. or according to taste
Water	$\frac{1}{2}$ cup

METHOD

1. Wash the potato, apply $\frac{1}{4}$ tsp. salt and keep aside for 10 minutes.
2. Wash the cashews and grind to a fine paste. Keep aside.
3. Heat the oil in a wok.
4. Sauté the potato till light golden brown in colour. Drain excess oil and keep aside.
5. Lower the flame and add the cloves, cardamom and cinnamon.
6. Add the ginger paste, turmeric, chilli and cumin powders. Fry till the oil separates. Add the tomato puree and cashew paste and fry for a minute more.
7. Add the water, potato, peas and raisins.
8. Bring the gravy to a boil. Lower the flame, add the diced paneer, and allow to simmer till the potato pieces are tender.
9. Check and adjust the seasoning and quantity of gravy.
10. Pour the ghee over it just before serving.
11. Serve with luchi.

CHINGRI MAACHHER MALAI CURRY

INGREDIENTS

Prawns	500 g
Creamed coconut	1 cup or a 200 g tetrapack
Ginger paste	1 tsp.
Green chillies	5-6; slit length-wise
Green cardamom	4-5
Clove	2-3
Cinnamon	1 inch piece
Turmeric powder	1½ tsp.
Oil	3 tbsp.
Salt	2 tsp.
Sugar	1 tsp.
Water	½ cup

METHOD

1. Clean, devein and wash the prawns.
2. Marinate with 1 tsp. salt and turmeric powder for 30 minutes.
3. Blend together the creamed coconut and water and keep aside.
4. Heat the oil in a wok.
5. Fry the prawns on a high flame till they change colour. Drain excess oil and keep aside.
6. To the same oil, add the cardamom, cloves and cinnamon and fry for half a minute.
7. Add the ginger paste and fry for another minute.
8. Add the coconut milk and green chillies, salt and sugar and bring to a boil.
9. Add the prawns. Cover and cook on a low flame till the prawns are cooked and the gravy thickens. Check the seasoning.
10. Serve hot with fried rice.

◆ ◆ ◆

TOMATO AMSHOTTOR CHAATNI

This is one variation of the popular tomato chutney.
You will get the sweet ampapad at any Bengali grocery shop or fruitseller.

INGREDIENTS

Tomato	250 g; washed and chopped
Amshotto/Ampapad	100 g; cut into ½ inch pieces
Raisins	10 g
Panch phoran	¼ tsp.

Salt	$\frac{1}{4}$ tsp.
Sugar	3 tbsp. or to taste
Oil	$\frac{1}{2}$ tsp.

METHOD

1. Heat the oil in a wok and add the panch phoran.
2. When they splutter, add all the ingredients.
3. Cover and cook on a low flame till the tomatoes are cooked. Stir occasionally to prevent sticking/burning.
4. Remove cover, check the seasoning and consistency of the chutney.
5. Serve chilled in summer or at room temperature in winter.

◆ ◆ ◆

NOTUN GURER PAYESH

This is a winter-time favourite because 'Notun Gur' or jaggery from the date palm is available only in this season. Good gur is available in the market from around end-December. The quality of the gur is determined from its texture. Good gur will be granular and always slightly soft – even when refrigerated.

INGREDIENTS

Milk	2 litres
Rice (Basmati/Govindbhog)	1 fistful
Sugar	2 tbsp.
Notun Gur	200-250 g

METHOD

1. Wash and soak the rice in water.
2. Boil the milk till it is reduced to half its original quantity. You must continuously stir the milk to get a thick, homogenous consistency.
3. Add the rice. Simmer till the rice is cooked. Stir frequently.
4. Add the sugar, stirring till it is completely dissolved.
5. Add approximately $\frac{3}{4}$ of the gur, and stir constantly till it dissolves and mixes well with the milk.
6. Check the sweetness. Add the remaining gur if required, or according to taste.
7. Chill and serve.

An All-Fish Menu

If you are planning a party and want to serve only fish-based Bengali fare, then try out this meal combination. This meal can be served when good quality hilsa is available, which is generally between February and October.

Pulao	Pulao
Bhaat	Boiled Rice
Maachher Fry	Fish Fries
Chholar Dal	Bengal Gram Dal
Tangra Maachher Jhaal	Tangra Fish Curry (dry)
Bhaapa Ilish	Steamed Hilsa
Anarosher Chaatni	Pineapple Chutney
Kheer Komola	Kheer with Orange

PULAO

This is my mother-in-law's recipe, and it is one of the best pulaos I've ever had.

INGREDIENTS

Basmati rice	250 g
Ghee	3 tbsp.
Cinnamon	1 inch piece
Green cardamom	5-6; bruised
Nutmeg	powdered; 1 pinch
Bay leaf	1
Raisins	15 g
Almond	15 g; slivered
Salt	1 tsp.
Sugar	1 tbsp. or to taste
Turmeric powder	$\frac{1}{4}$ tsp.
Water	3 cups

METHOD

1. Clean, wash and soak the rice for 1 hour. Drain out the water and spread out the rice to dry.
2. Blend 2 tbsp. ghee, the turmeric powder and salt with the rice and keep aside for at least 1 hour.
3. Heat the remaining ghee in a heavy bottomed or non-stick pan.
4. Add the cardamom, cinnamon, nutmeg and bay leaf, and sauté for a minute.
5. Add the rice and sauté for another 3-4 minutes.
6. Add the water, raisins and almond – keeping aside a little for garnishing.
7. Cook until the rice is done and all the water is absorbed. Stir occasionally with a fork.
8. Garnish with the remaining raisins and almonds and serve hot.

MAACHHER FRY

Ah! The Bengali fish fry has a distinct flavour all its own.

INGREDIENTS

Fish Fillet 500 g; preferably bhetki

For the marinade:

Onion paste	4 tbsp.
Ginger paste	2 tbsp.
Garlic paste	1 tbsp.
Lemon	1
Green chilli paste	1 tsp. (or according to taste)
White vinegar	1 tbsp.

For the coating:

Egg	1; beaten
Salt	1 tsp.
Bread crumbs	250 g
Refined oil	For deep-frying

METHOD

1. Wash the fish well.
2. Marinate with the juice of the lemon for 15 minutes.
3. Wash again and dry the fillets on paper towels.
4. Squeeze out the juice from the onion, ginger and garlic pastes.
5. Marinate with salt, vinegar, chilli paste and the onion/ginger/garlic juice for 3-4 hrs or overnight in the fridge.

To prepare the fries:

1. Dip each fillet in the egg and coat well with bread crumbs.
2. Keep in the fridge for at least 3-4 hrs before frying.
3. Heat oil in a frying pan.
4. Fry on a medium flame till golden brown.
5. Remove and drain excess oil on paper towels.
6. Arrange in a serving dish, garnish with wafers and lemon wedges.
7. Serve hot with tomato ketchup/mustard sauce with the pulao.

CHHOLAR DAL

This dal is usually served with luchi or fried rice.

INGREDIENTS

Bengal gram dal	100 g
Green chillies	3-4; slit length-wise
Coconut	1 tbsp.; finely chopped + 1 tbsp.; grated
Ginger paste	1 tsp.
Aniseed	$^1/_2$ tsp.; ground to a fine paste
Oil/Ghee	1 tbsp.
Cumin seeds	$^3/_4$ tsp.
Bay leaf	1
Salt	To taste
Sugar	2 tsp. or to taste

METHOD

1. Wash the dal well and pressure cook with 1 $^1/_4$ cup water (allow 3 whistles).
2. Heat the oil/ghee in a wok.
3. Add cumin seeds and bay leaves.
4. Add the chopped coconut and fry on a low flame till golden brown.
5. Add ginger paste and fry for a minute, add aniseed paste and fry for another minute.
6. Add the dal, green chillies, salt and sugar.
7. If required, add water to get the desired consistency. This is a thick dal.
8. Bring to boil, lower flame and let it simmer for a couple of minutes.
9. Garnish with grated coconut and serve hot with luchi or pulao and fish fry.

◆ ◆ ◆

TANGRA MAACHHER JHAAL

Bengalis eat a variety of small fish – prepared in various ways – normally dry and spicy. Tangra is of two kinds – the seawater and fresh water varieties. The latter is preferable, as it is more tasty.

INGREDIENTS

Tangra	500 g; small /medium sized
Potato	2 medium sized cut into thin fingers
Onion	2 medium sized; finely chopped
Tomato	2 large; finely chopped
Ginger	1 tsp.; finely chopped or grated
Garlic (optional)	1 tsp.; finely chopped
Green chillies	6-8; slit length-wise
Fresh coriander	2 tbsp.; chopped
Onion seeds	$^1/_4$ tsp.
Turmeric powder	1 tsp.
Cumin powder	1 tsp.
Chilli powder	$^3/_4$ tsp.
Mustard oil	4 tbsp.
Salt	To taste
Sugar	1 tsp. or according to taste
Water	$^3/_4$ cup

METHOD

1. Wash the fish well and dry on paper towels. Apply 1 tsp. salt and $^1/_2$ tsp. turmeric powder and keep aside for 30 minutes.
2. Wash and drain the potato. Add $^1/_2$ tsp. salt and keep aside for 10 minutes.
3. Heat 2 tbsp. oil in a wok.
4. Sauté the potato, in batches, for a couple of minutes.
5. In the same oil fry the fish in batches on a high flame, to a golden brown colour. Drain the excess oil and keep aside.
6. Throw away any residual oil. Heat the remaining oil.
7. Add the onion seeds.
8. Add the onions and fry till soft and transparent.
9. Add the grated ginger, garlic, remaining turmeric powder, cumin and chilli powders and fry on a low flame till well fried.
10. Add the chopped tomatoes, and $^1/_2$ tsp. salt. Cover and allow to cook till the tomatoes are soft.
11. Remove the cover, add the potato and continue to fry till the oil separates.
12. Add the water, 2-3 green chillies, salt and sugar. Check and adjust the seasoning.
13. Cover and cook till the potatoes are cooked.
14. Add the fish and cook, uncover for 3-4 minutes, turning the fish over once.
15. Garnish with sliced green chillies and fresh coriander, and serve hot with plain rice.

BHAAPA ILISH

Another classic from my mother-in-law's 'Opar Bangla' cuisine! A most unusual combination of spices which gives it an exclusive flavour.

INGREDIENTS

Hilsa	1 kg; cut cross-sectionally
Onion seeds	1 tsp.
Black pepper (whole)	2 tsp.
Cumin seeds	4 tsp.
Turmeric powder	1 tsp.
Salt	$1\frac{1}{2}$ tsp.
Green chillies	6-8; slit length-wise
Mustard oil	1 tbsp.
Banana leaf – optional or if available	1 or 2 depending on the size

METHOD

1. Clean, wash and dry the fish. Apply 1 tsp. salt and 1 tsp. turmeric powder and keep aside for 10 minutes.
2. Wash the whole masala. Grind all three to a fine paste along with $\frac{1}{2}$ tsp. salt and 2 green chillies.
3. Apply this paste to the fish, making sure all the pieces are well coated, and let it marinate for 30 minutes.
4. Put the fish in a tightly lidded container. Pour 2 tsp. mustard oil and 2-3 green chillies. Steam in a steamer/large pan of boiling water for 20-25 minutes. Check if the fish is cooked. If required, steam for a few minutes more.
5. Line a flat serving dish with banana leaf. Transfer the fish to the serving plate using a flat spoon, taking care not to break them.
6. Garnish with the remaining mustard oil and green chillies and serve hot with plain rice.

◆ ◆ ◆

ANAROSHER CHAATNI

This is one of my favourite chutneys learnt from my mother.

INGREDIENTS

Pineapple	1 large; grated
Raisins	25 g
Coconut (optional)	2 tbsp.; grated
Panch phoran	$^1/_2$ tsp.
Red chilli (whole)	1
Salt	$^1/_2$ tsp.
Sugar	3 tbsp. or according to the sourness of the pineapple
Oil	$^1/_2$ tsp.

METHOD

1. Heat the oil in a wok and add the panch phoran and red chilli.
2. When they splutter, add all the ingredients except the coconut.
3. Cover and cook on a low flame till the pineapple is cooked. Stir occasionally to prevent sticking/burning.
4. Remove cover and check on the seasoning and consistency of the chutney.
5. Add 1 tbsp. grated coconut, mix well and remove from fire.
6. Garnish with the remaining coconut and serve chilled.

◆ ◆ ◆

KHEER KOMOLA

INGREDIENTS

Milk	2 litres
Sugar	3 tbsp.
Orange	2

METHOD

1. Boil the milk till it is reduced to half of the original quantity. Add the sugar and keep stirring till the sugar dissolves completely.
2. Remove from fire, check and adjust the sweetness and chill.
3. Peel and flake the oranges into very small pieces and chill.
4. Add the orange to the thickened milk just before serving. Keep aside a little orange for garnishing.
5. Pour into a serving bowl, garnish with orange flakes and serve.

Variation: In summer, replace orange with diced, chilled mangoes.

Chhutir Diner Bishesh Aahar

Weekend or Holiday Cooking

This section is dedicated to weekend/holiday culinary pursuits, because this is when one has the leisure and mood to indulge in more elaborate and experimental cooking.

Menu I

This is a traditional menu, suitable for the winter months.

Bhaat	Boiled Rice
Motor Daler Paturi	Matar Dal with Vegetables
Palong Shaaker Ghonto	Spinach with Potato and Brinjal
Chingri Maachh Bhaapey	Steamed Prawns
Ranga Aloor Chaatni	Sweet Potato Chutney

Potol Bhaja

Pulao

Maachher Fry

Luchi

Pabda Maachh Shorshe

Kosha Mangsho

Tomator
Chaatni

Chhanar
Dalna

Chingri Maachher
Malai Curry

Bhaapa Ilish

Roshogollar Payesh

Chholar Dal

MOTOR DALER PATURI

This a very tasty dish, though a trifle time consuming to prepare, but worth the effort.

INGREDIENTS

Matar/Chana Dal	100 g
Cauliflower	$\frac{1}{2}$ of a small one; finely diced
Cabbage	$\frac{1}{2}$ of a small one; finely shredded
Beans	50 g; diced
Potato	1 large; diced
Peas	$\frac{1}{2}$ cup
Mustard oil	3-4 tbsp.
Salt	To taste
Sugar	1 tsp.

Grind together:

Coconut	4 tbsp. grated
Green chillies	3-4
Black mustard	2 tbsp.

METHOD

1. Wash and soak dal overnight. Then grind in a blender to make a fine paste.
2. Add the vegetables and the ground masala to the dal.
3. Heat 2 tbsp. oil in a heavy bottomed frying pan (preferably a non-stick one).
4. Pour the dal mixture, spread evenly, cover and cook on a low flame.
5. Turn over when the dal sets. Check occasionally to see if it is cooked through. Insert a fork or knife. If it comes out clean then you will know that it is done.
6. When done, brush the surface with 1 tbsp. oil and turn it over to brown. Brown the other side in a similar way.
7. Cut into wedges and garnish each wedge with 2-3 drops of mustard oil.
8. Serve hot with plain rice.

PALONG SHAAKER GHONTO

INGREDIENTS

Spinach	500 g; coarsely chopped
Potato	2 large; chopped into 1 inch cubes
Brinjal	1 large; chopped into 1 inch cubes
Green chillies	3-4 chopped
Bay leaves	2
Cumin seeds	$\frac{1}{3}$ tsp.
Cumin powder	1 tsp.
Heeng bori	$\frac{1}{2}$ cup (available at Bengali grocery shops)
Refined oil	4 tbsp.
Salt	To taste
Sugar	2 tsp. or to taste

METHOD

1. Wash all the vegetables separately and drain well.
2. Add $\frac{1}{2}$ tsp. salt to the potato and brinjal, mix well and keep aside for 10 minutes.
3. Heat 3 tbsp. oil.
4. Fry the bori till deep golden brown in colour. Drain excess oil and keep aside.
5. Heat 1 tbsp. oil in a wok.
6. Add the cumin seeds and bay leaves.
7. When the seeds crackle, add the potato and brinjal.
8. Sauté on a medium flame for 3-4 minutes or till the vegetables begin to brown.
9. Add the cumin powder and fry for another couple of minutes.
10. Add the spinach and cook for a couple of minutes on a high flame.
11. Add the green chillies and mix well.
12. Cover and cook till the vegetables and spinach are tender, stirring occasionally.
13. Remove the cover and cook on a high flame till the water has dried, stirring all the while.
14. Add salt and sugar to taste.
15. Garnish with coarsely crushed bori.
16. Serve hot with plain rice.

◆ ◆ ◆

CHINGRI MAACHH BHAAPEY

This is another delicious and exclusive Bengali preparation – prawns cooked with coconut and mustard.

INGREDIENTS

Prawns	500 g; small size
Coconut	1; grated
Yellow mustard seeds	2 tbsp.
Green chillies	4-5
Mustard oil	1 tbsp.
Salt	To taste
Turmeric powder	$\frac{1}{2}$ tsp.

METHOD

1. Clean, devein and wash the prawns.
2. Apply 1 tsp. salt and the turmeric powder and keep aside.
3. Grind together the coconut, mustard seeds, 2 green chillies and $\frac{1}{2}$ tsp. salt to a fine paste.
4. Add this paste, mustard oil and remaining green chillies to the prawns, mix well and keep aside for 30 minutes.
5. Put the prawns with the marinade in a container with a tight-fitting lid.
6. Steam it in a pressure cooker or steamer for 30 minutes.
7. Transfer to a serving bowl. Garnish with green chillies and 1 tsp. mustard oil and serve hot with plain rice.

◆ ◆ ◆

RANGA ALOOR CHAATNI

This is a very tasty chutney – typical Bengali fare.

INGREDIENTS

Sweet potato	250 g; diced into $\frac{1}{4}$ inch cubes
Panch phoran	$\frac{1}{2}$ tsp.
Red chilli (optional)	1
Roasted cumin powder	$\frac{1}{2}$ tsp.
Tamarind	1 ball; the size of a large lemon
Salt	$\frac{1}{2}$ tsp.
Sugar	3 tbsp.
Oil	1 tsp.

METHOD

1. Wash and boil the sweet potato in $\frac{1}{2}$ cup water till very soft. Remove from flame, retaining the water.
3. Soak the tamarind in $\frac{1}{2}$ cup of water.
4. Heat the oil in a wok.
5. Add the panch phoran and red chilli (if desired).
6. Add the sweet potato (with the water), salt and sugar and bring to a boil.
7. Let it simmer till the chutney acquires a paste-like consistency.
8. Lower the flame and add the pulp extracted from the tamarind.
9. Check and adjust the seasoning.
10. Pour into a serving bowl and cool to room temperature/chill depending on the season.
11. Garnish with roasted cumin powder and serve.

◆◆◆

Menu II

Another Sunday or holiday special in practically every Bengali household is 'Mangsho Bhaat' or mutton curry and rice. Sometimes the meal is literally this – rice and lots of mutton curry.

Bhaat	Rice
Musoor Dal aar Maachh Bhaja	Masoor Dal with Fried Fish
Mangsher Jhole	Mutton Curry
Aamer Tok	Mango Chutney

◆ ◆ ◆

MAACHH BHAJA

This is a slight variation from the common way of frying fish – another of my mother's recipes.

INGREDIENTS

Fish (Rohu/Katla)	500 g; or as desired
Onion/Ginger paste	1 tbsp.
Chilli powder	$\frac{1}{2}$ tsp.
Gram flour (besan)	2 tbsp.
Salt	1 tsp.
Turmeric powder	$\frac{1}{2}$ tsp.
Mustard oil	for frying

METHOD

1. Clean and wash the fish. Drain well.
2. Apply salt, turmeric powder, chilli powder and the juice of the onion/ginger paste. Marinade for 30 minutes.
3. Sprinkle the gram flour over the fish and mix well so that all the pieces are coated.
4. Heat the oil in a frying pan.
5. Fry the fish on a medium flame till cooked through and golden brown in colour.
6. Serve hot with rice and dal.

MANGSHER JHOLE

A favourite Sunday dish – try it out!

INGREDIENTS

Mutton (front leg)	500 g
Potato	4 large or 8 small
Onion	150 g
Ginger	1 inch piece
Garlic	6-8 cloves
Chilli powder	1 tsp.; or according to taste
Turmeric powder	$^3/_4$ tsp.
Green cardamom	3-4
Cinnamon	1 inch piece
Salt	1 $^1/_2$ tsp.
Sugar	2 tsp.; more (4 tsp.) if you are used to the taste
Mustard oil	4 tbsp.
Water	1 cup or depending upon the gravy required

METHOD

1. Clean and wash the meat and drain well.
2. Blend together the ginger, garlic and approximately 100 g of onion.
3. Finely chop the remaining onion.
4. Marinate the meat, onion, ginger, garlic paste, turmeric and chilli powders, salt and 2 tbsp. mustard oil for an hour.
5. Peel the potato and cut in half if large, else keep them whole.
6. Heat the remaining oil in a pressure cooker.
7. Fry the chopped onion till crisp and golden brown. Drain and keep aside.
8. Lower the flame and add the sugar. Keep stirring till all the sugar is dissolved and the oil turns red.
9. Add the cardamom and cinnamon and fry for half a minute.
10. Add the meat along with the marinade and fry on a high flame till the masala is well fried and the oil separates. This will take about 30-35 minutes.
11. Add the potato and water. Check and adjust the seasoning.
12. Pressure cook for 7 minutes on a low flame after the first whistle.
13. Garnish with the fried onions and serve hot with plain rice.

AAMER TOK

This cooling mango chutney is just the right thing to have after the rich, spicy mutton curry!

INGREDIENTS

Raw mango	2
Sugar	4 tbsp.
Salt	tsp.
Black mustard seeds	1 pinch
Oil	$^3/_4$ tsp.
Water	4 cups

METHOD

1. Peel, slice and wash the mangoes.
2. Heat the oil in a wok.
3. Add the mustard seeds.
4. When they splutter, add the mangoes.
5. Add the water, salt and sugar.
6. Bring to a boil. Lower the flame and allow it to simmer till the mangoes are cooked. Check sweetness and add sugar if still sour.
7. Serve chilled.

◆ ◆ ◆

Weekend Fare

This is another combination, suitable for a weekend lunch or dinner.

Pulao	Pulao
Mangsher Chop	Mutton Chops
Kosha Mangsho	Dry Mutton Curry
Anarosher Chaatni	Pineapple Chutney
Roshogollar Payesh	Kheer with Rasgullas

◆ ◆ ◆

MANGSHER CHOP

INGREDIENTS

Fine mutton mince	500 g
Potato	1 kg; boiled and mashed
Onion	250 g; finely chopped
Ginger	$1\frac{1}{2}$ inch piece; ground to a fine paste
Garlic	6-8 cloves; ground to a fine paste
Salt	To taste
Sugar	1 tsp.
Cumin powder	2 tsp.
Chilli powder	$\frac{3}{4}$ tsp.
Garam masala powder	$\frac{3}{4}$ tsp.
Turmeric powder	$\frac{1}{2}$ tsp.
Bread crumbs	For coating
Egg	2
Oil	For deep-frying

METHOD

1. Wash and squeeze out the water from the mince.
2. Heat 3 tbsp. oil in a wok.
3. Add the chopped onion and fry till transparent.
4. Add the ginger and garlic paste, all the masalas except the garam masala and fry on a low flame till cooked well.
5. Add the mince and fry well. Cover and cook till done. Sprinkle a little water if necessary.
6. Remove from fire and allow to cool.
7. Prepare the potato by adding salt and blending well.
8. Remove from flame and allow to cool.

To make the chops:

1. Divide the mince and potato separately into 10 equal portions.
2. Flatten one portion of potato in your palm. Place one portion of mince in the centre. Wrap the potato around the mince and shape into croquettes.
3. Beat the eggs in a bowl.
4. Dip each chop in egg, then coat with the bread crumbs and put away in a paper-lined tray.
5. Refrigerate for at least 4-5 hrs or overnight.
6. Heat oil in a deep yok.
7. Deep fry till deep golden brown.
8. Serve hot with ketchup.

◆ ◆ ◆

KOSHA MANGSHO

This mouth-watering preparation of mutton is one of my greatest favourites!

INGREDIENTS

Mutton (leg portion)	500 g
Yoghurt	$^3/_4$ cup
Onion	100 g; finely chopped
Ginger paste	4 tsp.
Garlic paste	4 tsp.
Tomato	2 large; finely chopped
Coriander powder	4 tsp.
Cumin powder	3 tsp.
Turmeric powder	1 tsp.
Chilli powder	2 tsp.
Mustard oil or Ghee	4 tbsp.
Salt	To taste
Sugar	2 tsp. or according to taste
Garam masala	2 tsp.

To make the 2 tsp. Garam Masala, grind together:

Cloves	6
Green cardamom	10
Cinnamon	1 inch piece
Bay leaf	1
Black peppercorn	10

METHOD

1. Clean and wash the mutton.
2. Marinate the mutton with yoghurt, 2 tsp. salt and $^1/_2$ tsp. turmeric powder for 30 minutes.
3. Heat the oil/ghee in a pressure cooker.
4. Add the onions and 1 tsp. garam masala and fry till onions are well browned.
5. Add the marinated mutton and cook for 5 minutes.
6. Add the ginger and garlic pastes, coriander powder, cumin powder, chilli powder, remaining turmeric powder and tomatoes.
7. Fry well till the masala is cooked and the oil separates.
8. Close the lid and cook on high flame. Lower the flame after the first whistle. Cook for 7 minutes.
9. Garnish with the remaining garam masala and serve hot with pulao.

ROSHOGOLLAR PAYESH

INGREDIENTS

Milk	1 litre
Sugar	2 tbsp.
Rasgulla	8-10 medium sized
Cardamom powder	$^3/_4$ tsp.

METHOD

1. Boil the milk till it is reduced to half of the original quantity. Add the sugar and keep stirring till the sugar dissolves completely.
2. Add the rasgullas and let it simmer for about 5 minutes.
3. Remove from fire, add $^1/_2$ tsp. cardamom powder and mix well.
4. Garnish with the remaining cardamom powder and serve chilled.

◆ ◆ ◆

Byasto Diner Ranna
Meals for a Week Day

This section has some meal combos for working days. The menus are simple, and so are the recipes. The menus have been drawn up keeping in mind the fact that the working wife/mother is short on time and energy.

Week Day Menu I

Here is the first of the 'Working Day' menus.

Bhaat	Plain rice
Kaacha Mooger Dal	Moong Dal
Paatla Maachher Jhole	Fish Curry

KAACHA MOOGER DAL

INGREDIENTS

Moong dal (yellow)	$^{3}/_{4}$ cup
Water	2 cups
Lime	1; cut in wedges
Green chillies	4-5
Ginger	1 tsp.; finely grated
Salt	To taste
Cumin seeds	$^{1}/_{3}$ tsp.
Bay leaves	2
Oil	$^{1}/_{2}$ tsp.

METHOD

1. Wash the dal well.
2. Pressure cook the dal. Allow 2 whistles on a high flame.
3. Remove the pressure cooker from the fire and allow it to cool.
4. Heat oil in a wok
5. Add cumin seeds and bay leaves.
6. When the seeds crackle, add the dal, green chillies and salt.
7. Bring to boil. Lower the flame, add grated ginger and let it simmer for 2 -3 minutes.
8. Serve with plain rice and lemon wedges.

◆ ◆ ◆

PAATLA MAACHHER JHOLE

This is the most common preparation for fish, ideal for everyday eating, as it is neither oily nor spicy and easy to prepare.

INGREDIENTS

Fish (Rohu/Katla/Telapiya)	500 g (approx.); cleaned and washed
Potato	2 medium; cut into fingers
Turmeric powder	1 tsp.
Coriander powder	1/2 tsp.
Chilli powder	1/2 tsp.
Salt	To taste
Mustard oil	2 tbsp.
Onion seeds	A pinch
Green chillies	3-4; slit length-wise
Coriander leaves	1 tbsp.; chopped
Water	3/4 cup – or according to the gravy required

METHOD

1. Apply 1/2 tsp. turmeric powder and 1 tsp. salt to the fish and keep aside for 10 minutes.
2. Apply 1/2 tsp. salt to the potato and keep aside for 5 minutes.
3. Heat 1 tbsp. oil in a wok.
4. Fry the fish in batches on a medium flame till light golden brown. Add more oil if required.
5. Throw away any leftover oil.
6. Make a paste of the remaining turmeric powder and coriander powder with a little water and keep aside.
7. Heat the remaining oil in a wok.
8. Lower the flame and add the onion seeds. When they splutter, add the potatoes and sauté for 3-4 minutes.
9. Add the masala paste and fry for a couple of minutes.
10. Add the water, salt to taste, green chillies and bring to boil.
11. Cover and allow to simmer till the potatoes are cooked through.
12. Add the fish and cook uncovered, on a low flame, for 3-4 minutes or till the fish is cooked.
13. Garnish with fresh coriander and serve hot with plain rice.

WEEK DAY MENU II

Bhaat	Plain rice
Musoor Dal	Masoor Dal
Potol Bhaja	Fried Parwal
Dimer Jhaal	Egg Curry

POTOL BHAJA

INGREDIENTS

Parwal	2 or 3 per person
Salt	To taste
Oil	For deep-frying

METHOD

1. Scrape the parwal skin and chop off the two ends.
2. You can either cut each parwal in two (length-wise) or leave it whole. In the latter case, make 3 rows of little gashes along the length of the parwal.
3. Wash well, drain, apply 1 tsp. salt and keep aside for 20 minutes.
4. Heat oil in a wok.
5. Fry the parwal in batches on a medium flame till they are well-browned and cooked through.
6. Drain excess oil on kitchen towels and serve hot as an accompaniment with rice and dal.

◆ ◆ ◆

DIMER JHAAL

An uncommon yet delicious preparation from my mother-in-law's collection! This dish is hot – so eat with care.

INGREDIENTS

Eggs	As desired
Potato	2 medium; cut in longish strips (as for French fries)
Whole red chillies	4
Garlic	$\frac{1}{2}$ a pod
Salt	To taste
Sugar	To taste
Refined oil	3 tbsp.
Water	$\frac{1}{2}$ cup

METHOD

1. Wash the potatoes well, apply $\frac{1}{2}$ tsp. salt, and keep aside for 10 minutes.
2. Boil the eggs. Cool and shell them.
3. Grind the garlic and chillies to a fine paste. Heat oil in a wok.
4. Add the potatoes and fry on a medium flame till they are half cooked.
5. Add the chilli-garlic paste and cook on a low flame till the masala is fried and the oil separates.
6. Make 4 gashes on the white of each egg. This will allow the spices to penetrate.
7. Add the eggs and fry for 2-3 minutes more.
8. Add the water and check and adjust the seasoning.
9. Cover and cook till the potatoes are soft. Remove the cover and cook for a couple of minutes. This dish has very little gravy.
10. Serve hot with plain rice.

Kicchu Niramish Ranna

Some Vegetarian Meals

Here is the first of the vegetarian menus.

MENU I

Aloo Korola Sheddho	Mashed Potato with Bitter Gourd
Begoon Bhaja	Fried Aubergines

ALOO KOROLA SHEDDHO

INGREDIENTS

Potato	4 medium
Bitter Gourd	1 large
Mustard oil	1 tsp.
Green chillies	2-3; coarsely chopped
Salt	To taste

METHOD

1. Wash the vegetables and place in pressure cooker with 1 cup water.
2. Cook on a high flame. Remove from fire after 4 whistles.
3. Cool the cooker. Peel the potatoes and mash them along with the bitter gourd.
4. Add the mustard oil, salt and green chillies.
5. Blend well. Serve with hot plain rice.

BEGOON BHAJA

INGREDIENTS

Brinjal	1 large
Salt	To taste
Turmeric powder	$^{1}/_{2}$ tsp.
Chilli powder	$^{1}/_{4}$ tsp.
Sugar (optional)	$^{1}/_{2}$ tsp.
Gram flour (besan)	2 tbsp.
Oil	For frying

METHOD

1. Cut the brinjal down the middle and then into $^{1}/_{2}$ inch thick slices.
2. Wash well and drain.
3. Add salt, sugar, turmeric and chilli powders, and coat the slices well. Keep aside for 5 minutes.
4. Heat oil in a frying pan.
5. Coat the brinjal slices with besan and fry in batches on a medium flame till cooked and golden brown.
6. Drain the excess oil.
7. Serve hot with rice and dal.

◆ ◆ ◆

Menu II

Gola Bhaat	Rice
Dal Shiddho	Boiled Masoor Dal
Aloo Bhaatey	Mashed Potato

GOLA BHAAT

INGREDIENTS

Rice	250 g
Peas	$\frac{1}{2}$ cup shelled
Cauliflower	1 small; cut in florets
Carrots	2; cut in 1 inch cubes
Salt	$\frac{1}{2}$ tsp.
Water	5-6 cups

METHOD

1. Wash the rice and vegetables.
2. Put all the ingredients in a heavy-bottomed pan.
3. Cook the rice in the usual way, till all the water is absorbed.
4. This rice is meant to be overcooked and a little pasty.
5. Serve hot with the dal and mashed potato.
6. Add ghee (oodles of it!) and salt to taste.

◆ ◆ ◆

DAL SHIDDHO

INGREDIENTS

Masoor Dal	150 g
Onion (optional)	1 large; sliced
Salt	1 tsp.
Water	1 $^{1}/_{2}$ cups
Green chillies	2-3; slit length-wise

METHOD

1. Wash the dal.
2. Put all the ingredients – except green chillies – in a pressure cooker.
3. Allow 2 whistles on a high flame.
4. Allow the cooker to cool to room temperature.
5. Add green chillies and heat through.
6. Serve hot with gola bhaat.

◆ ◆ ◆

ALOO BHAATEY

INGREDIENTS

Potato	500 g
Onion	1 medium; finely chopped
Green chillies	3-4; coarsely chopped
Salt	To taste
Mustard oil	1 tsp.
Fresh coriander	1 tbsp.; chopped

METHOD

1. Pressure cook the potatoes.
2. Peel and mash them.
3. Combine with all the remaining ingredients.
4. Serve with the gola bhaat and dal.

Grishmokaaler Ranna

Summertime Fare

During the hot summer and humid monsoon months, you will just not be able to cook or enjoy rich, spicy food. Here are preparations which are just right for these seasons. Easy to cook and digest!

Let us take a look at this menu.

Menu I

Bhaat	Plain Rice
Teetar Dal	Moong Dal with Bitter Gourd
Aloo Posto	Potato with Khus Khus
Tomato diye Murgi	Chicken Curry with Tomato

TEETAR DAL

INGREDIENTS

Moong dal (yellow)	½ cup
Water	2 cups
Bitter gourd	1 medium sized; cut into thin slices
Lime	1; cut in wedges
Green chillies	4-5
Ginger	1 tsp.; finely grated
Salt	To taste
Black mustard seeds	A pinch
Bay leaf	1
Oil	4 tsp.

METHOD

1. Heat 3 tsp. oil in a wok.
2. Apply salt to the bitter gourd and then fry in batches till crisp. Keep aside. Discard any leftover oil.
3. Put the dal and water in a pressure cooker and cook.
4. Allow 2 whistles on a high flame.
5. Remove from fire and allow it to cool.
6. Heat 1 tsp. oil in a wok.
7. Add mustard seeds and bay leaf.
8. When the seeds crackle, add the dal, fried bitter gourd, green chillies and salt.
9. Bring to boil. Lower the flame, add grated ginger and let it simmer for 2-3 minutes.
10. Serve hot with plain rice and lemon wedges.

Variation: Bottle gourd can also be added. Cut in 1 inch cubes and pressure cook along with the dal.

◆ ◆ ◆

ALOO POSTO

One of the most popular Bengali dishes. Posto or khus khus is an integral part of the cuisine of West Bengal.

INGREDIENTS

Potato	300 g; peeled and cut into $\frac{1}{2}$ inch cubes
Khus khus	4 tbsp.; ground to a fine paste
Turmeric powder	$\frac{1}{4}$ tsp.
Green chillies	4-6; slit
Oil	1 tbsp.
Salt	To taste
Sugar	1 tsp. or to taste

METHOD

1. Wash and drain the potatoes. Rub in 1 tsp. salt and keep aside for 10 minutes.
2. Heat oil in a wok.
3. Add the potato, turmeric powder, and stir on a high flame for 3-4 minutes.
4. Add the green chillies, salt and sugar. Cover and cook on a low flame.
5. Stir occasionally. If the potatoes tend to stick to the bottom, add a little water.
6. When the potato are half done, add the khus khus paste, check and adjust seasoning and cook till the potatoes are cooked. If required you may add a little more oil.
7. Garnish with green chillies and serve with plain rice.

◆ ◆ ◆

TOMATO DIYE MURGI

This is not a typical Bengali recipe, but one from my mother's collection.

INGREDIENTS

Chicken	1 kg; cut into 12 pieces
Potato	2 large; cut into 8 pieces each
Onion	2 large; thinly sliced
Ginger	1 tbsp.; finely chopped
Garlic	2 tbsp.; finely chopped
Tomato	2 large; finely chopped
Green chillies	5-6; slit length-wise
Green cardamom	4; bruised
Clove	2
Cinnamon	1 inch piece
Peppercorn	6-8; crushed
Refined oil	2 tbsp.
Salt	To taste
Sugar	To taste

METHOD

1. Clean, wash and dry the chicken pieces.
2. Wash the potatoes and apply $^{3}/_{4}$ tsp. salt and keep aside.
3. Heat oil in a wok.
4. Sauté the potatoes till lightly browned. Drain the oil and keep aside.
5. In the same oil add the cardamom, clove, cinnamon and peppercorns.
6. Add the onion and garlic and fry till the onions are well browned.
7. Add the chopped ginger and green chillies and fry on a low flame for 3-4 minutes.
8. Add the chicken pieces and brown them on a high flame.
9. Add the chopped tomatoes, salt and sugar and fry for 3-4 minutes.
10. Add the potatoes, cover and cook on a low flame till the chicken and potatoes are tender. Adjust the gravy as desired.
11. Serve hot with rice.

BEAT THE SUMMER HEAT

Bhaat	Boiled Rice
Aloo Potol diye Maachher Jhole	Fish Curry with Potato and Parwal
Toker Dal	Dal with Green Mango

ALOO POTOL DIYE MAACHHER JHOLE

INGREDIENTS

Fish (Rohu/Katla)	500 g
Potato	2 large; cut into 8 pieces each
Parwal	8; peeled and cut in halves
Ginger paste	1 tsp.
Cumin seed	A pinch
Bay leaf	2
Turmeric powder	1 tsp.
Cumin powder	½ tsp.
Coriander powder	1 tsp.
Chilli powder	½ tsp.
Fresh coriander	1 tbsp.; chopped
Green chillies	4-5; slit length-wise
Salt	To taste
Sugar	1 tsp.
Mustard oil	4 tbsp.
Water	1 cup – or according to gravy required

METHOD

1. Wash the fish and vegetables well and drain for about 10 minutes.
2. Apply ½ tsp. turmeric powder and 1 tsp. salt to the fish and keep aside for 15 minutes.
3. Apply 1 tsp. salt to the potato and parwal and keep aside for 10 minutes.
4. Heat 2 tbsp. oil in a wok.
4. Lightly fry the fish in batches on a high flame, taking care not to break them.
6. Discard any oil left in the wok. Heat 2 tbsp. fresh oil.
7. Add cumin seeds and bay leaves.
8. Add the potato and parwal and sauté for 3-4 minutes on a medium flame.
9. Add the ginger paste, turmeric, cumin, coriander and chilli powders and fry for a few minutes. Sprinkle a little water if the masala tends to burn or stick.
10. When the masala is fried, add the water, salt, sugar and green chillies and bring to boil.
11. Cover and allow to simmer on a low flame till the vegetables are almost cooked.
12. Add the fish and cook till the vegetables are fully cooked.
13. Garnish with fresh coriander and serve hot with plain rice.

Variation: In winter you can substitute parwal with cauliflower.

TOKER DAL

This dal is made only in summer when green mangoes are available. This dal is actually a coolant! It is eaten at the end of the meal.

INGREDIENTS

Matar dal	100 g; available in Bengali grocery shops
Green mango	1 medium size; peeled and sliced
Mustard seed (black)	A pinch
Red chilli (dry)	1-2
Oil	$\frac{1}{2}$ tsp.
Salt	To taste
Sugar	1 tbsp. or to taste
Water	$1\frac{1}{2}$ cups

METHOD

1. Cook the dal in a pressure cooker with the water. Allow 3 whistles.
2. Heat the oil in a wok.
3. Add the mustard seeds and red chilli. When they splutter, add the mango and fry for a minute.
4. Add the dal. Check and adjust the seasoning and bring to a boil. The quantity of sugar will depend on individual taste, but it is meant to be sweet and sour.
5. Cover and cook on low flame till the mango slices are soft.
6. Serve with rice at room temperature.

Note: In case you are unable to get matar dal, you may use red masoor dal. Also, toker dal is served at room temperature, not hot.

◆ ◆ ◆

Sheetkaaler Ranna
Cooking in Winter

Winter is the season when the markets are full of a large variety of vegetables and fish, and, also – appetite picks up alarmingly after a long and dreary summer. You want to cook whatever you lay your eyes on! So here are some meals for those exciting months!

◆ ◆ ◆

MENU I

Try out this combination for a Sunday lunch in winter.

Bhaat	Boiled Rice
Lal Shaak Bhaja aar Kasundi	Fried Red Saag with Mustard Sauce
Narkoler Dudh diye Maachh	Fish in Coconut Milk
Tomator Chaatni	Tomato Chutney

LAAL SHAAK BHAJA AAR KASUNDI

INGREDIENTS

Red saag	1 big bunch – approx 500 g
Onion seed	A pinch
Red chillies (dry)	2
Green chillies (optional)	2-3
Garlic	3-4 cloves; chopped
Oil	2 tsp.
Salt	To taste
Kasundi	Available at all Bengali groceries

METHOD

1. Finely chop the saag and wash very well.
2. Heat oil in a wok.
3. Add the onion seeds and red chillies.
4. When they splutter, add the garlic and sauté for a couple of minutes.
5. Add the saag and green chillies.
6. Fry for a few minutes and then cover and cook on a medium flame till it is cooked.
7. Remove the cover and cook on a high flame, stirring all the while, till most of the water dries up.
8. Now add the salt, mix well and cook on a low flame to allow the salt to penetrate and the remaining water to dry up.
9. Serve with hot plain rice and kasundi.
10. Kasundi is added according to individual taste.

◆ ◆ ◆

NARKOLER DUDH DIYE MAACHH

INGREDIENTS

Fish (Rohu/Katla/Pomfret/Topshey)	500 g
Potato	2 medium; cut into fingers
Onion	1 medium; finely sliced
Ginger paste (fresh)	$\frac{1}{2}$ tsp.
Coconut milk	1 cup (see basic preparations) or a 200 g tetra pack
Milk	$\frac{1}{2}$ cup
Green cardamom	5-6, bruised
Cloves	2
Cinnamon	1 inch piece
Turmeric powder	1 tsp.
Cumin powder	$\frac{1}{2}$ tsp.
Green chillies	6-8; slit length-wise
Salt	To taste
Sugar	1 tsp.
Oil	4 tbsp.

METHOD

1. Wash the fish and potatoes well and drain for about 10 minutes.
2. Apply $\frac{3}{4}$ tsp. turmeric powder and 1 tsp. salt to the fish and keep aside for 15 minutes.
3. Apply $\frac{1}{2}$ tsp. salt to the potatoes and keep aside for 10 minutes.
4. Heat 2 tbsp. oil in a wok.
5. Lightly fry the fish in batches on a high flame, taking care not to break them.
6. Discard any oil left in the wok. Heat 2 tbsp. fresh oil.
7. Add the cardamom, cloves and cinnamon.
8. Add the potatoes and and sauté for 3-4 minutes on a medium flame.
9. Add the ginger paste and cumin powder and fry for a few minutes. Sprinkle a little water if the masala tends to burn or stick.
10. When the masala is fried, add the milk, salt, sugar and half of the green chillies and bring to boil.
11. Cover and allow to simmer on a low flame till the potatoes are almost cooked.
12. Add the fish and and coconut milk and adjust seasoning. Let it simmer, uncovered, till the fish and potatoes are cooked.
13. Garnish with green chillies and serve hot with plain rice.

MENU II

Bhaat	Rice
Aloo Phoolkopir Chorchori	Dry Cauliflower/Potato Curry
Tel Koi	Fish Curry

ALOO PHOOLKOPIR CHORCHORI

INGREDIENTS

Cauliflower	1 large; cut into medium sized florets
Coconut	½
Mustard seeds (yellow)	1 tbsp.
Green chillies	6-8 or according to taste
Onion seed	½ tsp.
Oil	1 tbsp.
Salt	To taste
Sugar	2 tsp. or according to taste

METHOD

1. Wash and drain the cauliflower. Apply 1 tsp. salt and keep aside.
2. Grind together the coconut, mustard seeds, 2-3 green chillies and ½ tsp. salt to a fine paste.
3. Heat the oil in a wok.
4. Add the onion seeds.
5. Add the cauliflower and stir on a high flame for 3-4 minutes.
6. Lower the flame, cover and let it cook. If the vegetable tends to stick to the bottom, sprinkle a little water and stir.
7. When the cauliflower is almost done, add the coconut-mustard paste, a few more green chillies, salt and sugar.
8. Cover and cook till the masala is cooked and the cauliflower is tender yet crunchy.
9. Remove the cover and fry for a couple of minutes more.
10. Garnish with green chillies and serve hot with plain rice.

Variation: You can substitute cauliflower with 500 g parwal. Peel and make ½ inch deep cuts (like X) at both ends.

TEL KOI

This is a delicious, though a trifle high on oil, preparation of fish. Koi is not easily available, so you may substitute it with telapiya or even fresh-water tangra.

INGREDIENTS

Fish (Koi/Telapiya)	500 g; whole
Tomato	2 large; grated
Green chillies	5-6
Onion seeds	1 pinch
Chilli powder	$\frac{1}{2}$ tsp.
Turmeric powder	1 $\frac{1}{4}$ tsp.
Mustard oil	4 tbsp.
Salt	To taste
Sugar	1 tsp. or to taste
Water	$\frac{1}{2}$ cup

METHOD

1. Wash and drain the fish.
2. Apply 1 tsp. salt and 1 tsp. turmeric powder and keep aside for 30 minutes.
3. Heat 1 $\frac{1}{2}$ tbsp. oil in a frying pan.
4. Fry the fish in batches on a high flame. Drain and keep aside.
5. Throw away any leftover oil and heat the remaining oil in a flat-bottomed pan.
6. Add the onion seeds. Lower the flame and add the turmeric and chilli powder and 2-3 tsp. water.
7. Fry the masala for 2-3 minutes.
8. Add the tomato, 2-3 green chillies and $\frac{1}{2}$ tsp. salt and fry till the tomatoes turn mushy.
9. Add the fish, water, salt to taste and sugar, and bring to a boil.
10. Lower the flame, cover and allow to simmer till the fish is cooked and water dries. The gravy is supposed to be of oil – as the name suggests – and not water.
11. Garnish with green chillies and serve hot with plain rice.

A Winter Lunch

This meal is best enjoyed on a winter afternoon or a rainy day because this food will, without fail, knock you out for a couple of hours! It can also be cooked when you are not in the mood for a 4-5-course meal. Just some fries as accompaniment is sufficient. Here I have made a more elaborate combination, in case you wish to serve this meal for guests.

Khichuri	Kedgeree/Khichri
Begoon Bhaja	Fried Aubergines
Ilish Maachh Bhaja	Fried Hilsa
Tomator Chaatni	Tomato Chutney

◆ ◆ ◆

KHICHURI

Bengali khichuri is very different from the North Indian variety – definitely not a patient's diet! It is more akin to the 'Tehri' of Uttar Pradesh.

INGREDIENTS

Rice	1 cup
Moong dal (yellow)	½ cup; roasted
Musoor dal	½ cup
Onion	2 large; sliced
Ginger	1 tbsp.; grated
Tomato	2 large; chopped
Green chillies	4-5
Onion (for garnishing)	2 large; finely sliced

Vegetables to put in khichuri (optional):

Potato	4 large; peeled and halved
Green peas	1 cup (shelled)
Cauliflower	8-10 florets
Green cardamom	6
Cloves	4
Cinnamon	2 inch piece
Bay leaves	2
Jeera powder	2 tsp.
Haldi powder	$^1/_2$ tsp.
Oil	2 tbsp.
Ghee	2 tbsp.
Salt and sugar	To taste
Water	6 cups (same cup used for measuring the rice and dal)

METHOD

1. Roast the moong dal till light golden brown.
2. Wash the rice, dal and vegetables separately and drain well.
3. Heat the oil in a heavy-bottomed pan.
4. Fry the onions (for garnishing) in small batches till brown and crispy.
5. In the same oil add the garam masala and bay leaves,.
6. Add the onions and fry till they are soft and transparent.
7. Add the ginger and fry for 3-4 minutes more.
8. Add the rice and dal. Fry for 3-4 minutes on a low flame.
9. Add the turmeric and cumin powder and fry for 3-4 minutes more.
10. Add the tomatoes and fry for 2-3 minutes.
11. Add the vegetables, 5 cups water, salt and sugar. The chillies may be added whole or slit – according to taste.
12. Bring to boil on a high flame.
13. Cover and let it simmer on a low flame, stirring the contents occasionally.
14. If required, add more water, $^1/_2$ cup at a time.
15. If the khichuri is cooked but too watery, remove lid and keep on a low flame till the water dries.
16. Garnish with fried onion slices and green chillies.
17. Serve hot with ghee and fries.

ILISH MAACHH BHAJA

The tastiest fish – most Bengalis would agree. Tastes good any which way it is prepared. Fried hilsa with khichuri is a favourite combination – in fact a complete meal in itself.

INGREDIENTS

Hilsa	$\frac{1}{2}$ kg – or as desired
Salt	1 tsp.
Turmeric powder	$\frac{1}{2}$ tsp.
Mustard oil	2 tbsp.

METHOD

1. Clean and wash the fish. Drain well.
2. Apply salt and turmeric powder and keep aside for 15 minutes.
3. Heat the oil in a frying pan.
4. Fry the fish on a medium flame till golden brown in colour and cooked through.
5. Serve hot.

Variation: Rohu or katla can also be used if hilsa is not available.

◆ ◆ ◆

Jolkhabar
Snacks

Bengali cuisine has a fairly large storehouse of snacks as well. Evening tea is usually accompanied with 'jolkhabar' or snacks. Here are a few.

Luchi Torkari	Luchi with Dry Potato Curry
Aloo Dimer Bora	Egg and Potato Balls
Cheerer Pulao	Pressed Rice Pulao
Kucho Nimki	Flour Crispies
Elo Jhelo	Flour Crispies (sweet)
Motor Shutir Kochuri	Green Pea Patties

◆ ◆ ◆

ALOOR TORKARI

INGREDIENTS

Potato	500g; peeled and cut in 1/2 inch cubes
Oil	1 tbsp.
Green chillies	4
Onion Seeds	$^1/_2$ tsp.
Salt	To taste
Sugar	2 tsp. or according to taste

METHOD

1. Wash and drain the potatoes. Add 1 tsp. salt and keep aside for 5 minutes.
2. Heat the oil in a wok.
3. Add the onion seeds.
4. Add the potatoes and fry till they begin to brown.
5. Add the sugar and green chillies.
6. Cover and cook on a low flame stirring occasionally.
7. Check and adjust seasoning. Sprinkle a little water if required.
8. When the potatoes are cooked through, uncover and cook till all the liquid dries up.
9. Pour into a serving dish.
10. Serve hot with the luchis.

Note: 'Luchi Torkari' is a favourite Sunday breakfast as well.

◆ ◆ ◆

ALOO DIMER BORA

INGREDIENTS

Potato	500 g; boiled and mashed
Egg	2
Fresh coriander	1 tsp.; finely chopped
Onion	1medium; finely chopped
Green chillies	3-4; finely chopped
Salt	To taste
Oil	For deep-frying

METHOD

1. Mix together the potatoes, yolk of two eggs, and all other ingredients.
2. Beat the egg whites till stiff.
3. Heat oil in a wok.
4. Form balls with the potato mixture – the size of a big lemon. Dip in the egg white and fry till light golden brown.
5. Drain excess oil on paper towels.
6. Arrange in a serving dish, garnish with onion rings, and serve hot with tomato ketchup.

CHEERER PULAO

INGREDIENTS

Pressed Rice (Chewda)	100 g
Potato	2 large; peeled and cut in $^1/_2$ inch cubes
Peas	$^1/_2$ cup - shelled
Onion	1 large; finely sliced
Green chillies	2-3; chopped
Green cardamom	6
Cinnamon	1 inch piece
Peppercorn (optional)	6-8
Oil	2 tbsp.
Salt	To taste
Sugar	2 tsp.

METHOD

1. Wash and drain the potatoes. Apply 1 tsp. salt and keep aside for 10 minutes.
2. Heat oil in a wok.
3. Add the cardamom, cinnamon and peppercorns. Fry for 30 seconds.
4. Add the potato and sauté on high flame till lightly browned.
5. Add the peas, salt, sugar, green chillies and $^1/_2$ cup water. Cover and cook on a low flame till the vegetables are tender.
6. Wash the pressed rice and immediately drain out the water.
7. Add to the vegetables and mix well.
8. Check and adjust the seasoning.
9. Cook uncovered on a medium flame for 2-3 minutes.
10. Serve hot.

Variation: You may substitute the peas with 50 g fried/roasted peanuts or omelette cut into thin strips.

◆ ◆ ◆

KUCHO NIMKI

INGREDIENTS

Refined flour	250 g
Ghee/Oil (for dough)	2 tbsp
Salt	2 tsp
Sugar (optional)	1 tsp
Lemon (optional)	1
Water	4 tbsp
Onion seeds	2 tsp
Oil	For deep-frying

METHOD

1. Combine refined flour, 2 tbsp oil, salt, sugar and onion seeds and mix well.
2. Add juice of 1 lemon and water, and knead into a stiff dough.
3. Divide the dough into 5 equal portions.
4. Roll each portion with a little dry flour into thick chapati-sized discs.
5. With a sharp knife, cut each disc into ½ inch X 1 ½ inch strips.
6. Heat oil in a wok. Fry the strips in small batches on a medium flame till crisp and golden in colour. Stir constantly so that the strips do not stick.
7. Serve hot or at room temperature.
8. You can make these in your spare time and keep in airtight containers as they will keep for many days.

◆ ◆ ◆

ELO JHELO

INGREDIENTS

Refined flour	250 g
Ghee/oil (for dough)	2 tbsp.
Sugar	2 tsp.
Water	4 tbsp.
Oil	For deep-frying

For the syrup:

Sugar	250 g
Water	2 cups

METHOD

1. Combine the refined flour, 2 tbsp. ghee/oil, sugar and water to make a stiff dough.
2. Make the sugar syrup by boiling together the sugar and water till slightly thick. Keep aside.
3. Divide the dough into equal portions – each the size of a small lemon.
4. Roll out each portion with a little dry flour into thin discs.
5. With a sharp knife, make gashes in the disc, leaving intact $\frac{1}{2}$ inch all around. Roll the disc (like you would make a paratha roll) and press together the two ends so that the roll does not open out.
6. Heat oil in a wok.
7. Fry a few at a time, on a medium flame, till golden brown. Drain excess oil.
8. Dip in the sugar syrup and ensure that each piece is well coated.
9. Place them on an oiled tray/plate and let the sugar syrup dry completely.
10. You can store them in airtight containers after they are completely dried.
11. They keep for upto 2 weeks.

◆ ◆ ◆

MOTOR SHUTIR KOCHURI

A most delicious snack this one is!

INGREDIENTS

Refined flour	300 g
Ghee/Oil	4 tbsp.
Water	4½ tbsp.
Green peas	500 g; shelled
Asafoetida	½ tsp.
Chilli powder	½ tsp.
Cumin-chilli powder	2 tsp. (see basic preparations)
Salt	To taste
Sugar	2 tsp. – or to taste
Oil	For deep-frying

METHOD

1. Combine the refined flour, 1 tsp. salt, 2 tbsp. ghee/oil, water and knead into a stiff dough. Refrigerate for 2 hrs.
2. Grind the peas to a fine paste.
3. Heat 2 tbsp. ghee/oil in a wok.
4. Lower the flame and add the asafoetida.
5. Add the pea paste, sugar, salt to taste and chilli powder. Mix well and cook for 5-6 minutes on a low flame, stirring all the while so that it does not burn.
6. Add the cumin-chilli powder and cook for another 2 minutes.
7. Remove from fire and keep aside.
8. Divide the dough into equal portions, each the size of a medium lemon.
9. Shape each portion into a disc about 2 inches in diameter.
10. Make a well in the middle, add adequate stuffing and cover it.
11. Roll each into a disc about 3 inches in diameter.
12. Deep fry on a low flame till golden brown in colour.
13. Drain excess oil and serve hot.

Helpful Hints

i. Try to cook in non-stick cookware. Not only do you use less oil, you also eliminate the problem of sticking/burning while cooking. It is especially useful when cooking fish.

ii. Chutneys and desserts are served chilled. So prepare them a day before, or on the morning of the party so that you have sufficient time to chill them.

iii. Fries and chops are best prepared one day in advance and refrigerated, as they are time consuming.

iv. When boiling eggs, add 2 tsp. salt to the water. This prevents the eggs from cracking.

v. To remove the 'fishy' smell from the fish, marinate it with lime juice and salt for half an hour. Wash the fish and dry well before cooking.

vi. When cooking fish, make sure they are well thawed and at room temperature at the time of cooking.

vii. When frying fish before making the curry, heat the oil well, then fry quickly on a high flame. This will prevent the fish from breaking in the curry.

viii. Fish is almost always fried before being made into a curry. Fry the fish in as little oil as possible. Discard any leftover oil after frying the fish, and make the curry in fresh oil.

ix. It is preferable to use mustard oil for cooking fish and most preparations of chicken and mutton. Mustard oil imparts a distinctive flavour and colour to the dish. Where mustard oil is unsuitable, I have mentioned the oil to be used as refined oil.

x. Before freezing fish, be sure to wash it well and drain out the water. Also, apply 2 tsp. salt and 2 tsp. turmeric powder for every kilogram of fish. Mix well and freeze in portions that you will cook for one meal. This helps to retain its taste for 2-3 weeks. Repeated thawing and re-freezing will make the fish lose its taste and freshness.

xi. Here is a special tip about hilsa. This fish loses its taste and oils if washed too much. So remove the scales and other dirt from the stomach of the fish first, then wash it well only once under running water.

xii. Store 'Notun Gur' in a plastic or glass container in the refrigerator. It will keep for a year.

Basic Preparations

Given below are some basic preparations which you may find handy.

CUMIN CHILLI POWDER

1	tsp. cumin seeds
2	red chillies

1. Roast the ingredients on a griddle till they are crisp to the touch.
2. Grind and store in an airtight container.
3. This quantity makes almost 2 tsp. of powder.

PANCH PHORAN

1	tsp. cumin seeds
1	tsp. fenugreek seeds
1	tsp. fennel seeds
1	tsp. black mustard seeds
1	tsp. onion seeds

1. Mix and store in an air tight container.
2. Use when required.

COCONUT MILK

1	Coconut

1. Grind the coconut to a fine paste and pass through a muslin cloth to get the first (thick) extract.
2. Boil the coconut paste with an equal amount of water to get the second (thin) extract.
3. It will keep in the refrigerator for 2-3 days.

DAHI (YOGHURT)

1	litre milk
1	tbsp. yoghurt

1. Heat the milk till it is warm to the touch.
2. Stir in the youghurt.
3. Pour into an earthen/ceramic pot.
4. Cover and keep in a warm place to allow it to set.
5. Yoghurt takes longer to set in winter than in summer.

Glossary

Given below are the most commonly required terms:

ENGLISH	HINDI / BENGALI

SPICES

Aniseed	Saunf / Mouri
Asafoetida	Hing
Bay Leaf	Tejpata
Basil	Tulsi
Bengal gram	Chana / Chholar dal
Cardamom (green)	Chhoti Elaichi / Elach
Carom seeds	Ajwain / Jowan
Cinnamon	Dalchini / Darchini
Cloves	Laung / Lobongo
Cumin	Jeera
Coriander leaves	Dhania patta / Dhoney pata
Fenugreek	Methi
Garlic	Lashun / Roshun
Gram flour	Besan / Beshon
Mace	Javitri
Mustard seeds	Sarson / Shorshe
Nutmeg	Jaiphal
Onion seeds	Kalonji / Kalojire
Poppy seed	Khus-khus / Posto
Refined Flour	Maida
Turmeric	Haldi / Holud

VEGETABLES

Aubergine	Brinjal
Baingan	Begoon
Bitter gourd	Karela
Bottle gourd	Lauki / Lau
Cabbage	Bandh Gobi / Bandha Kopi
Capsicum	Shimla Mirch / Capsicum
Carrots	Gajar
Cauliflower	Phool Gobi / Phool Kopi
Cucumber	Kheera / Shosha
Greens	Saag / Shaak
Jackfruit	Kathal / Echor
Lady's fingers	Bhindi
Mint leaves	Pudina Patta
Papaya	Papita / Pepey
Pumpkin	Kaddu / Kumro
Green / Raw banana	Kachcha Kela
Spinach	Palak / Palong Shaak
Sweet Potato	Shakarkandi / Ranga Aloo
Tamarind	Imli / Tetool

FRUITS & NUTS

Almond	Badam
Cashewnuts	Kaju Badam
Dates	Khajoor
Groundnut	Moonphali / Chinebadam
Orange	Santara / Komla Lebu
Papaya	Papita / Pepey
Pineapple	Annanaas / Aanarosh
Pistachio	Pesta
Raisin	Kishmish
Walnut	Akhrot
Watermelon	Tarbooz / Tormooj

Index

Recipe	*Page no.*